It had been a hot summer's day and it started to thunder
just as Mummy was tucking her young son into bed.
The boy was terrified and, in a shaky voice, asked,
'Mummy, would you stay with me in my room tonight?'
Mummy gave her little boy a big hug and said,
'I can't. I have to sleep in bed with Daddy.'
The little boy was silent for moment and then said,
'He's such a scaredy cat!'

Which is the best hand to write with?

Neither – it's better to use a pen!

'How was your exam?
Did you have any difficulty with the questions?'
'Not with the questions, but I did with the answers!'

2

The Green family returns from a holiday in Italy.
'Did you have a nice time there?' asks the neighbour.
'Fantastic!' replies Mr Green.
'And how did you find Rome?'
'Oh, easily,' replies Mr Green, 'we used the SatNav!'

3

Gerry has a new job as lighthouse keeper.
He returns home in the evening on the first Monday.
'I thought you'd be back on Saturday?'
says his wife. 'What happened?'
'They sent me away,' Gerry replies, glumly.
'Why?'
'Because I turned the light off when I went to bed.'

4

Lenny is having dinner with his Mum and Dad.
'Mum, pass me the bread,' he says.
Dad looks at Lenny crossly and says,
'Mum, PLEASE could you pass me the bread!'
'No, Dad,' says Lenny, 'I was first!'

5

A salmon is smoking a cigarette.
A starfish swims up to him and asks,
'Why are you smoking a cigarette?
Salmons don't smoke, do they?'
'Oh, but they do,' the salmon answers,
'when they want to become a smoked salmon!'

6

'I hardly slept a wink last night!' says Nick.
'Why not?' asks Chris.
'There was a gurdyglee on the roof.'
'A gurdyglee? What's that?'
'You don't seriously think I'm going to get out of bed
in the middle of the night and climb onto the roof
just to find out what a gurdyglee is, do you?'

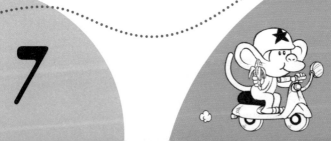

Will and Bert are standing on the roof of a huge skyscraper.
Will suddenly loses his balance and falls off the edge.
'Are you still alive?' Bert calls after him.
'Yes!' replies Will.
'Have you broken anything?'
'No!'
'How's that possible?'
'I'm still falling!'

8

'Did you know that ants are the most hard-working of all animals?
They work day and night and never have time off,' says Leo.
'That's not true,' replies Gary.
'When we go on holiday, they're there too!'

٩

'Mum?' asks Wally.
'Does anyone live on the Moon?'
'Of course, darling,' replies his mum,
'There's a light on every evening!'

10

Two rascals are waiting on a platform.
'Should we take this train?' asks one.
'I want to,' replies the other,
'but it won't fit into my pocket!'

11

The teacher asks, 'Who knows
which bird doesn't build its own nest?'
Bart answers, 'A cuckoo, sir!'
'Very good, Bart – and do you know
why it doesn't build its own nest?'
'Because it lives in a clock, sir!'

A thief breaks into Walter's house in the middle of the night.
Walter wakes to find him in his bedroom.
'Are you looking for something?' asks Walter.
'Money!' replies the thief.
'Oh, me too,' laughs Walter, 'can I help you look?'

'Well Steven, did you follow the doctor's advice?
A glass of hot milk first, then a hot bath?' asks Mum.
'I drank the glass of milk, Mum,' Steven replies,
'but I didn't manage to finish the bath!'

What always comes after a black cat?

Its tail!

15

Granddad asks Harry, 'So, boy, do you like going to school?'
'Yes, Granddad, I like going to school.
And I like coming home again.
I like the period in between much less!'

'I feel attracted to you,' one magnet says to another.

What did the gnome say when he bumped into another gnome?

'What a small world!'

17

Bert is as proud as punch when he finishes his first year
at school. 'Now I'm smarter than the teacher!' he shouts.
'How's that?' asks his mum.
'Well, I'm going up to the next year in September
but the teacher has to stay in this one!'

Two friends meet.
One has just returned from being on holiday.
The other asks, 'What did you see in Australia?'
'I don't know,' replies the first,
'I haven't looked at the photos yet!'

19

What frightens kangaroos the most?

Pickpockets!

20

Vick and Jeff find three bombs while they are digging a hole.
'We'll take the bombs to the police,' says Vick.
'What if one goes off?' asks Jeff, worried.
'Don't worry,' replies Vick. 'Then we'll just say
that we only found two!'

A man goes to visit his friend, who is playing chess with his dog.
'Incredible! Your dog can play chess! That's got to be
the most intelligent dog in the world!' he shouts.
'Hmm,' replies his friend. '"Most intelligent" is perhaps pushing
it a bit; he's lost three out of five games this morning!'

22

How can you tell which end is the tail and which is the head on an earthworm?

Tickle him; the end that laughs is the head!

23

Addressing the waiter, a man in a restaurant asks,
'What can you recommend for dinner?'
'To be honest, sir,' replies the waiter,
'I'd recommend dining at the restaurant across the street!'

**I have one arm, three heads and four legs.
What am I?**

A liar.

'Waiter! There is a slug in my salad!' says William.
'I'm very sorry, sir!' says the waiter.
'I didn't realise that you were a vegetarian!'

George goes to the doctor.
'Doctor, I don't know what's wrong with me.
I'm as tired as a dog in the morning. I could eat a horse in
the afternoon and I sleep like a bear at night!'
'Then you're better off going to the vet,' replies the doctor.

'Mum, a dog has just bitten my leg!' howls Chris.
'You poor thing! Did you rub anything on it?' asks his mother.
'No, he didn't like the taste!'

28

'Have you seen my new painting?' asks Ellen.
'It's so good that it'll bring tears to your eyes!'
'What have you painted?'
'A sliced onion!'

29

During the lesson Frances shouts,
'Vroom, vroom, vroom.'
The teacher says, 'If you do that one more time,
you're going to the headteacher's office.'
A little later Frances again shouts,
'Vroom, vroom, vroom.'
'Right,' says the teacher, 'go and stand in the corridor.'
Frances replies, 'I can't, miss, my petrol tank is empty.'

'Granddad?' asks Jolene, 'if you know where something is,
does that mean that you haven't lost it?'
'Of course,' replies Granddad.
'Great! I just dropped the house key
down the drain outside!'

31

Two new-born babies are lying
beside each other in a maternity ward.
'Are you a boy or a girl?' one baby asks the other.
'I'm a girl, what are you?'
'I don't know.'
'Pull up your blanket, so I can see,' says the girl.
'Ah, I see. You're a boy.'
'How do you know that?'
'You're wearing blue socks!'

A young tourist visits an old castle. The tour guide asks whether she has enjoyed the tour. The tourist says that she has, but she really wanted to see a ghost. The guide says that in all the time he has worked there, he has never seen a ghost. 'How long have you been working here?' asks the tourist. 'Three centuries, give or take a year,' replies the guide.

33

A woman goes into a clothes shop.
'Hello, I would like to try on the dress in the window, please.'
The shop assistant turns bright red and asks,
'Are you sure you wouldn't prefer to use
the changing room?'

Patrick is reading the telephone book.
His friend sits down beside him and asks, 'Is it a good book?'
'Not bad,' replies Patrick. 'But it has too many characters.'

35

'I've lost my dog!' cries Eve.
'Put an advert in the newspaper, that will help,' says Jimmy.
'What's the point of that? My dog can't read!'

An old man is sitting opposite a young boy on the train.
Suddenly the old man says,
'You don't need to talk to me, boy, I'm deaf as a post!'
'I'm not talking,' shouts the boy,
'I'm chewing gum!'

37

'Granddad, would you like me to fetch your glasses?' asks Xander.
'Why? I don't need glasses to watch television!' replies Granddad.
'I think you do,' says Xander. 'You've been staring at the oven
for the past half hour!'

38

A man puts up ten 'Beware of the dog' signs in his garden.
His neighbour asks, 'What's with all the signs?
You only have a small dog?'
'Exactly,' replies the man.
'I don't want anyone to step on him!'

39

'Grandma, have you got good teeth?'
asks Nelly.
'Unfortunately not, love,' replies Grandma.
'Phew, that's good.
You can keep an eye on my sweets then!'

Two pirates bump into each other.
'Hey,' says one to the other,
'have you got a hook instead of a hand?'
'Yes,' replies the second pirate, 'I lost my hand
during a battle on the Galapagos Islands.'
'And the scar on your face? Did you get that there as well?'
'No, I was bitten by a mosquito, but I hadn't quite
got used to my hook by then!'

'Mum, may I go to Luke's party?' asks Melanie.
'OK, but only if you're polite. Don't run through the house and
don't squabble with Alex and Dimitri like the last time. Agreed?'
'But how am I supposed to have fun
if I can't do any of those things?'

'Dad, I went to the farm today!'
says Emma, proudly.
'There were lots of pigs and they talk
just like you do when you're asleep!'

Cowboy Billy steps into the saloon.
'Who has painted my horse green?!' he fumes.
A colossal man stands up from a table and rolls up his sleeves.
'That would be me. Do you have a problem with that?!'
'Er… no,' replies Billy.
'I wanted to ask you when you're coming to do the second coat.'

A mouse and an elephant are walking through the jungle.
The mouse starts to puff and pant.
'You can sit on my back if you're exhausted!' says the elephant.
'OK,' says the mouse.
'But we're switching after ten minutes!' says the elephant.

Daniel goes to a farm.
He asks the farmer's wife, 'Where is the farmer?'
'He's in the pig sty with the pigs.
You'll spot him easily – he's the one wearing the hat!'

A horse owner is angry that his horse
came last in the show jumping competition.
'Really! Couldn't you have jumped a bit higher?'
he yells at the jockey.
'Yes, I could,' the jockey replies,
'but I had to stay with the horse, didn't I?'

Two friends are playing together.
'Shall we play mummies and daddies?' asks one.
'No, that's boring. I don't feel like doing the dishes
while you sit in the armchair watching television!'

48

What do you call a boomerang that never comes back?

A stick.

'Jasper, I've told you a thousand times to put your hand
in front of your mouth when you cough!' says Mum.
'I tried, Mum, but it didn't help!'

50

'Dad,' Elliot asks his father, 'what would be worse?
If I'd broken my leg or if I'd broken a window?'
'If you'd broken your leg, of course,' answers Dad.
'Oh, then I can put your mind to rest,' says Elliot.
'I haven't broken my leg!'

At school the children had to write a story about an animal.
After marking the papers the teacher calls out to David,
'David, your story about your dog is word for word
the same as your twin sister's! Can you explain this?'
David replies: 'Of course, sir. We have the same dog!'

52

'You need to discipline your dog better,' says a passer-by to Ted.
'Why? What happened?' asks Ted.
'Whenever I start to sing, your dog starts to howl loudly!'
'Ah!' says Ted, 'But you started it, then!'

Sophie asks her granny, 'How old are you, Granny?'
'Oh, darling, I'm so old that I can't even remember!'
'Oh, but then you should look in your underwear,'
replies Sophie. 'Mine says, "age 6"!'

'Mum, when was I born?' asks Simon.
'On the 15th of November,' answers Mum.
'What a coincidence,' says Simon,
'that's the same day as my birthday!'

55

Fiona and her mother are at the zoo.
Fiona has never seen a peacock, so when passing a peacock run,
she says, 'Look, Mum, that turkey is in bloom!'

Peter takes a taxi home after a night out.
'That'll be twelve pounds, please,' says the driver.
'How much?!' complains Peter, 'I've only got ten pounds on me!
Could you drive back a bit, please?'

'Mum, why have you got grey hair?' asks Sophie.
Mum replies: 'I get a few more grey hairs
every time you're naughty.'
'Now I know why Grandma is so grey then,' says Sophie.

Two ghosts are flying through a house.
Suddenly, one says to the other,
'You've dropped a handkerchief!'
'No,' he replies, 'that's my son!'

'My father can stop ten cars with one hand!' boasts Peter
to his girlfriend. 'That's not possible!' she says.
'Oh yes it is – he's a traffic policeman!'

♥

Jerome comes out of school and says to his mum,
'Mum, I wish we had a round classroom.'
'Why's that?' asks his mum.
'If we had a round classroom,
I wouldn't have to stand in the corner.'

An angry woman walks into a launderette and exclaims:
'This is a disgrace! Look at this!' and holds out a handkerchief.
The launderette owner looks at the handkerchief and says,
'That looks like a very clean and well-ironed handkerchief
to me, madam. What is wrong with it?'
The woman replies: 'It was a tablecloth when
I brought it in here to be cleaned – that's what!'

A farmer is cycling through the village, with his horse walking
behind him. He is stopped by a police officer.
'Well,' says the officer, 'that's going to be a hefty fine!
You know your horse isn't allowed to walk freely
through the streets!'
'Blast it!' says the farmer, 'Has he jumped off
my baggage rack again?'

A man enters a pub, performs a double somersault and a double backflip, and lands gracefully on a barstool. The landlord looks at him, impressed, and asks: 'Where did you learn to do that?'
'I work in the circus. I'm an acrobat,' he replied.
A little later another man enters the pub, performs a triple somersault and a triple backflip, and lands gracefully on a barstool. Again, the landlord asks: 'And where did you learn to do that?'
'I work in the circus. I'm an acrobat.'
Ten minutes later another man walks into the pub, performs an extravagant run-up, a triple somersault, leaps over the landlord, lands on the ground, does a backflip and lands perfectly on a barstool. Gasping in amazement, the landlord says: 'Don't tell me, you work in the circus!'
The man replies: 'No, I tripped over the doormat!'

Two polar bears are walking through the desert.
One says to the other:
'It must have been really slippery here.
Look how much sand they've strewn!'

65

'Diana, you mustn't copy Norah's sums!'
says the teacher, sternly.
'But I'm not copying the sums, miss, only the answers!'

Tony has been dieting for the past few months.
His friend Mark asks him whether he's noticed a difference.
'Can you touch your toes yet?' he asks.
'Not touch them, no,' replies Tony, 'But I can see them again!'

'Why do bees have antennae, Wendy?' her little sister asks.
'I don't know,' she replies.
'To stir the honey!'

♥

'Mum, can I have a lolly?' asks Emma.
'No, sweetheart, you'll get holes in your teeth.'
'Oh, but I'll lick it, not bite it!'

♡

Stan is walking through the woods with his father.
'Can you hear that knocking sound?' asks his father.
'That's a woodpecker!'
'Why is he knocking?' asks Stan.
'He's eating worms, which live under the bark,' replies his father.
'Then it's odd that the worms open the door when he knocks!'

70

Leon shows his father his piggy bank.
'Dad, look how thin my pig is,' Leon moans.
'You're underfeeding him!'

71

Letitia goes to stay on her aunt's farm.
In the evening she watches as her aunt plucks a chicken.
'Aunty, do you always have to undress the chickens
before they go to bed at night?'

A family with two children is eating at a restaurant.
The children are served a bowl of soup. After a while, the boy
turns to his parents and says, 'There's a fly in my soup!'
They tell him to leave the soup, to which his little sister responds,
'I want a fly in my soup, too!'

Jeff and Simon are discussing the circus show they've just seen.
'I didn't think much of the knife thrower,' says Jeff.
'He threw about 20 knives at that girl, but all of them missed her!'

74

A visitor to the zoo sees one of the zoo keepers weeping.
'Dear man, whatever is the matter?' asks the visitor.
'Our elephant died last night,' sobs the keeper.
'Poor you. You must miss him a lot.'
'No, that's not it,' replies the keeper,
'I have to dig a huge hole to bury him in!'

75

Two men walk past a huge stone.
'What will I get if I lift up that stone?'
one asks, flexing his muscles.
'Backache!' replies the other.

A fly asks a centipede, 'Where is your wife these days?
I haven't seen her for weeks.'
'She's gone to buy shoes!'

A couple arrives at an airport after a long, tiring train journey.
The man sighs and says, 'I wish we'd brought the piano!'
'Why on Earth do you say that?' asks the woman.
'Because the plane tickets are on top of it!'

Why do gnomes always laugh when they're playing soccer?

Because the grass tickles their armpits!

79

'Benny, do you know how to catch a rabbit?' asks Larry.
'No,' answers Benny.
'You have to stand behind a tree and make carrot noises!'

The director of a circus receives a phone call. 'I'd like to come and work for you. I can sing, dance and play the violin,' says the caller. 'I'm afraid that's not enough to work in a circus, madam,' the director replies. 'So what else does a hippopotamus have to be able to do?' the caller replies.

A man calls the doctor and says,
'Doctor, my son has swallowed my pencil!
What should I do?'
'Write with a pen,' the doctor replies.

Why wouldn't the elephant use the computer?

Because he was afraid of the mouse!

How can you tell if an elephant has been in your refrigerator?

By the footprints in the butter!

Eva has been given a kitten for her birthday.
One evening the kitten falls asleep in front of the fire
and soon begins to purr. 'Mum! Mum!' wails Eva,
'she's too near the fire. She's starting to boil!'

84

A man goes to the library.
'I'll have a large portion of chips, a hamburger and a cola, please!'
'Sir, this is a library!' replies the librarian.
'Oh, sorry,' whispers the man. 'I'll have a large portion of chips,
a hamburger and a cola, please.'

What do you call a dinosaur that is sleeping?

A dino-snore!

**What do you get when you cross
a vampire and a snowman?**

Frost bite.

Jake and Pete are camping on the moors.
Jake wakes Pete in the middle of the night.
'Pete, look up at the stars and tell me what you see.'
'Well,' says Pete, 'I see millions of stars.'
'And what does that tell you?' asks Jake.
'That there are also planets between the millions of stars and that
there has to be life on at least one of those planets, just like on Earth!'
'No, you idiot!' replies Jake.
'It tells us that our tent has been stolen!'

'Which is more important for us, the Sun or the Moon?'
the teacher asks Quentin.
'The Moon, sir,' he replies.
'Why the Moon?'
'Because it gives off light when we need it – in the dark.
The Sun gives off light when we don't need it –
during the day!'

'If I were to give you two rabbits, Philip, and then another two,
how many rabbits would you have?' asks the teacher.
'Five!' replies Philip. 'How did you arrive at that number?'
asks the teacher. 'Surely you'd only have four?'
'Yes, sir, but I already have a rabbit at home!'

A small girl is sitting on the pavement in front of a house.
A man walks past and asks:
'Is your mother at home, child?'
'Yes, sir,' replies the child, politely.
The man rings the doorbell, but no one opens the door.
'Why is no one answering?' asks the man, slightly vexed.
'You said that your mother was home!'
'Yes, she is,' replies the girl. 'But I don't live here!'

The sales assistant in the shoe shop says to a customer,
'Your new shoes will probably pinch a little during the first few days.'
'That's OK,' says the customer.
'I won't be wearing them until next week!'

91

'Caroline,' says Lizzy,
'do you know what your belly button is for?'
'No,' replies Caroline.
'It's to put salt in,' says Lizzy,
'so you can sprinkle it on your boiled egg
when you have breakfast in bed!'

Three men have been shipwrecked on a desert island.
The men are very homesick. One day they are visited
by a mermaid, who says: 'Each of you may make a wish.'
The first man wishes to return home and suddenly finds himself
standing in his living room, at home. The second man wishes
to be at home as well and a moment later he is standing in his
garden, absolutely delighted to be back with his family again.
Only the third man remains, who sighs and says: 'Pfff, it's boring
here without those two. I wish they were back here again!'

The doctor says to his patient,
'The marks on your arm will disappear if you apply
this cream and don't play the trumpet for a year.'
The man leaves the practice and the doctor's assistant
turns to the doctor: 'What has playing the trumpet
got to do with those marks?'
'Nothing,' he replies, 'but he lives next to me and
I've had enough of listening to him play the trumpet!'

Emily sees her mum rubbing cream onto her face
and asks her why she's doing it.
'I'm doing it to stay beautiful,' she tells Emily.
In the evening she removes all the cream
from her face with a tissue.
'Oh, Mum,' says Emily, 'are you giving up already?'

Billy and Johnny go to stay at their grandma's.
Before getting into bed, they kneel in front of
the bed and start to pray.
In a very loud voice, Billy begins:
'I PRAY FOR A NEW BICYCLE,
I PRAY FOR A NEW IPOD
AND I PRAY FOR A PLAYSTATION!'
'Why are you shouting like that?' asks Johnny.
'God isn't deaf.'
'No,' replies Billy, 'but Grandma is!'

'Elsie, what an odd pair of stockings you're wearing!'
says her friend, Leah.
'One leg is yellow and the other is green!'
'Funky, aren't they?!' replies Elsie.
'I've got another pair just like them at home!'

97

The teacher catches Jordan cheating during a test.
'Jordan, that's the third time I've seen you looking
at your neighbour's paper!'
'Yes, sir, but it's not my fault his writing is so unclear!'

What's odd about parents?

First they teach you to walk and talk,
then later they tell you to, 'Sit down and be quiet.'

'Dad, can you write in the dark?' asks Peter.
'I think so,' replies his father. 'Why do you ask?'
'Because you have to sign my report!'

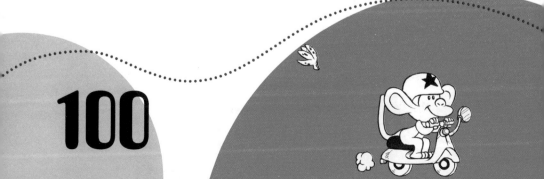

100

Two sardines see a submarine approaching.
One sardine says to the other, 'Look, tinned people!'

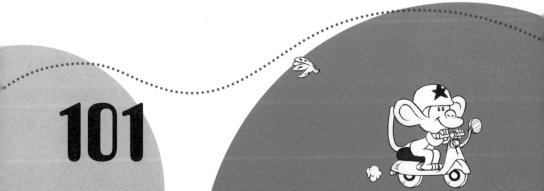

101

A cheapskate goes to a restaurant with
his family. When they've finished eating,
he asks the waiter for a box to put
the leftovers in, so he can take them home.
'For our dog,' he tells the waiter.
To which the children reply:
'Hooray! We're getting a dog!'

102

The teacher asks his pupils
'If 1+1=2 and 2+2=4, what is 4+4?'
'That's not fair, sir!' one boy replies.
'You answer the easy ones
and leave us with the hard one!'

103

A cowboy arrives in town on Friday. He rides out of town again on Friday two days later. How's this possible?

His horse is called 'Friday'.

'My dog can count,' says Derrick.
'Oh really?' James answers.
'Yes, when I ask him what four minus four is, he says nothing!'

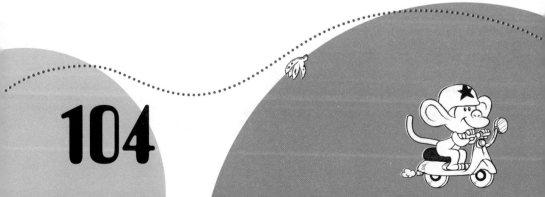

104

Johnny is at the lost and found office.
'Has anyone brought in a bicycle?' he asks.
'They sure have, young man. What colour?'
'Light blue, preferably,' replies Johnny.

105

A policeman stops Paul one evening
as he's cycling home from work.
'You have to dismount if your light
is not working, sir!'
'I've tried that,' says Paul,
'but it still doesn't work!'

What noise do hedgehogs make when they kiss?

'Ouch!'

How do you know if there's an elephant under your bed?

You can touch the ceiling.

Two flies are resting on a bald head.
One asks the other:
'Do you remember when we used
to play hide and seek here?'

108

Joseph brings his cat to the vet.
'What should I do, doctor?
My cat ate a bag of unpopped popcorn.'
To which the vet replies:
'I'd start with keeping him out of the sun!'

109

The teacher asks the pupils to name
five things that contain milk.
'Butter, cheese and three cows!' replies Damon.

What did one plate say to the other plate?

Dinner is on me!

Why do birds fly south in the winter?

Because it's easier than walking.

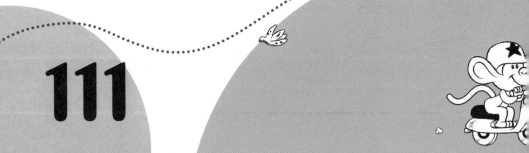

**What has a head,
one foot and four legs?**

A bed.

A smurf is walking through the park
when suddenly he trips over a stone
and bangs his head on a bench.
'Ouch!' he shrieks. 'Another blue mark!'

112

Two snakes meet in a swamp.
One snake says to the other: 'I hope I'm not venomous.'
'Why?' asks the second snake.
'Because I've just bitten my tongue!' he replies.

113

**What do you get if you cross
an elephant with a mole?**

A huge mess in your garden!

'Can someone tell me which liquid doesn't freeze?'
asks the teacher.
'Warm water, sir!' replies Gary.

114

What do you call a sheep without a head or legs?

A cloud!

115

'Why are you so short, Dad?'
'Because I'm afraid of heights, love!'

A city boy has found a summer job on a farm and has to milk cows for the first time in his life. He takes a stool and bucket into the meadow and returns several hours later, with an empty bucket.

'Why is your bucket still empty?' asks the farmer.

To which the boy indignantly replies, 'You have very stubborn cows – none of them would sit on the stool.'

'Why are you hiding all your old school reports?'
Helen asks her husband. 'As a precautionary measure of course.
The children are learning to read now!'

Brian has been asking his mother question after question.
Her patience is running thin.
'Brian, if you ask "why" one more time I'll get very cross!'
'Why, Mum?'

118

The teacher asks Jodie,
'What is the future tense of "I am tired"?'
Jodie answers, 'I am sleeping!'

Why do witches fly on broomsticks?

Because vacuum cleaners are too heavy.

'David!' yells his father.
'Either listen to what I say or go to bed
without having dinner – what's it to be?'
'That depends on what we're having!' his son replies.

Two matches are lying in hospital.
One match asks the other match,
'Why are you here?'
'Burnt head. You?'
'Broken leg.'

121

'Hey, Ella, shall we hide Daddy's slippers?' asks Nina.
'Yes!' replies Ella. 'Then we can learn a few more swear words!'

What is the height
of politeness?

Knocking before you open the fridge door.

How do you know that carrots are good for your eyes?

Have you ever seen a rabbit wearing glasses?

123

Which planet is married?

Saturn, it's the only one that wears a ring.

The teacher of a Year 4 class asks Amy if she can name
one important thing that didn't exist ten years ago.
'Me!' Amy replies.

124

Gertie and Sophie walk past a bakery.
They see a delicious cream cake in the window.
'Mmmmmmm,' says Gertie. 'I'd love a piece of that!'
'Are you bonkers?' asks Sophie. 'It's 60% fat!'
'Oh,' replies Gertie. 'I'll just eat the other 40% then.'

125

What type of paper floats in the sea?

A swimming certificate.

During a geography lesson, the teacher asks
the pupils which areas they think cannibals might live in.
'The coast, miss,' says Ted.
Amazed at his answer, the teacher asks him to explain.
'It's in our geography book, miss,' explains Ted.
'It says that the inhabitants live off the tourists!'

**What time was it when the elephant
sat on the garden fence?**

Time for a new one.

127

'Daddy! You're gonna be proud of me!
I was the only one who answered the teacher's question!'
'And what was the question?'
'It was, "Who put chewing gum on my chair?"'

Gerry is at the dentist.
'You don't need to drill,' he says,
'there's already a hole in my tooth!'

A horse and a man walk into a bar. The horse orders an apple
juice and the man orders a glass of water. The barman says,
'I have never seen a horse order an apple juice before!'
'Indeed,' says the man.
'Very strange. Normally he orders lemonade!'

129

Why can't you milk a mouse?

Because it's impossible to get a bucket underneath.

Two young dogs are visiting the city for the first time
and see a parking meter.
'Unbelievable,' says one dog to the other,
'You have to pay to pee here.'

Aiden is walking to the supermarket with his Grandma,
when he sees a 50 pound note lying on the ground.
'Grandma,' he asks, 'may I pick that up?'
Grandma replies, 'No, if it's on the ground, it's dirty.'
A little later he sees a 100 pound note lying on
the floor and asks, 'Grandma, may I have that?',
to which Grandma replies, 'No, if it's on the floor, it's dirty.'
Around the corner, Grandma slips on a banana skin on the ground.
'Help me up, Aiden,' she cries.
'No, Grandma,' Aiden replies.
'If it's on the ground, it's dirty!'

**How many letters are
there in the alphabet?**

11: t-h-e a-l-p-h-a-b-e-t.

'Tim, what do you want to be when you grow up?'
asks the teacher. 'Father Christmas, of course,
because he only has to work once a year!'

Adam and Eve are lying on the grass.
Eve asks Adam, 'You love me, don't you?'
Adam turns towards her, sighs and says,
'Of course dear, who else?!'

♥

Two bananas are lying in a bed.
One banana says to the other:
'Would you please lie straight!'

'Sir,' says Paul. 'I don't think I deserve a zero for my exam.'
'I know,' replies the teacher, 'but I couldn't give you less!'

How far can an elephant walk into the woods?

Until he reaches the middle.
From there on, he'd be walking back out again.

Two pairs of underpants are waiting
in the laundry basket to be washed.
One pair says to the other:
'Have you been on holiday? You look so brown!'

Why did the cat say 'woof'?

Because it was learning a new language.

●●●●●●●

Laura goes to bed and asks her mother,
'Mum, may I read until I fall asleep?'
'OK,' her mother replies. 'But not a minute longer!'

Two friends arrive at the doctor's.
One friend exclaims, 'Doctor, I've swallowed a frog.'
'And what's your problem?' the doctor asks his friend.
'It's my frog!' he replies.

137

John returns home from school. His mother asks,
'How was your day at school?' John replies, 'I was the only
one who could answer the teacher's question!'
'That's great!' says Mum, 'What was the teacher's question?'
John says, 'Who hasn't done the homework?'

**Why do people hold their hands above their eyes,
when they want to see far into the distance?**

Because they'd see nothing if they held their hands in front of their eyes.

139

A man is having dinner in a restaurant and sees
a hearing aid floating in his soup. He shouts,
'Waiter, there is a hearing aid in my soup!'
To which the waiter replies: 'Pardon?'

**What runs through cities and villages,
over mountains and past lakes, but doesn't move?**

The road.

140

Ethan goes to visit the doctor.
'Doctor,' he says, 'it hurts when I press my arm with my finger,
it hurts when I press my leg with my finger and it hurts when I
press my tummy with my finger! What could be wrong?'
'I see what the problem is,' says the doctor.
'Your finger is broken.'

Why did the kid cross the playground?

To get to the other slide.

How many books can you fit into an empty satchel?

One, because after that the satchel's no longer empty!

142

'Why are my teeth called milk teeth, Mummy?'
'Because you drink so much milk, darling.'
'Does Daddy have beer teeth then?'

'Waiter, what is that fly doing in my soup?'
'Hmm, backstroke I think, sir.'

During the maths lesson, the teacher proudly announces,
'Children, we're going to use calculators for our sums
from now on! So, if you have three calculators and
you buy four more, how many calculators do you have?'

144

Roy's mother asks him,
'So, have you been naughty at school again today?'
'No, Mum,' Roy replies. 'I didn't get the opportunity.
I had to stand in the corner all day.'

145

A man goes to the doctor and says,
'Doctor, I think I'm suffering from memory loss.'
'How long have you been troubled by this?' asks the doctor.
'By what?' he replies.

One friend says to the other,
'If you can guess how many biscuits are in my lunchbox,
you can have them both!'

A mother monkey says to her son,
'OK, you can go and play inside.
But no people business, please!'

What did the gaming fanatic's gravestone read?

Game over.

A man goes to collect his car from the garage.
'We weren't able to repair your brakes,' says the mechanic,
'So we've made the horn louder and the lights brighter!'

148

An elephant and a mouse are walking through the desert in the burning sun. The mouse has been walking in the elephant's shadow all day. After a while, the mouse asks the elephant, 'Would you like to walk in my shadow for a while?'

149

**What do you get if you cross
a vampire and a teacher?**

Lots of blood tests!

'How come you broke your leg?'
'Do you see that pothole?'
'Yes.'
'I didn't.'

'Do you know the "I thought so" joke?'
'No.'
'I thought so!'

A trainee pilot contacts the control tower
and asks for clearance to land.
'OK,' replies the air traffic controller.
'Please provide your position and height.'
'Uh...,' says the pilot. 'I'm on the plane
and I'm 5 foot, 10 inches tall.'

151

What has two humps and is found at the North Pole?

A lost camel!

A granddad says to his grandson, 'I used to be as small as you, you know.' His grandson laughs, 'You must have looked very funny with such a long beard and glasses!'

'Why have you put your teddy bear in the freezer, Noah?' asks Mum.
'Because I'd rather have a polar bear, Mum!' he replies.

153

David is given a sweet by his grandma.
'What do you say?' asks Grandma.
'Another one!' replies David.

'Why haven't you learnt the vocabulary list?' asks the teacher.
'I couldn't learn last night, sir, because I had a sore throat.'
'But surely you can learn if you have a sore throat?'
'No, sir, I can't. I always learn out loud.'

**What do you call a snowman
who has had too much sun?**

A puddle.

155

Why was Danny fired from the M&Ms factory?

Because he threw all the M&Ms with a 'W' on them in the bin!

'How far do your homing pigeons fly?'
'Very far!'
'And do they always find their way home?'
'Always, because I crossed them with a parrot.
So if they get lost, they can always ask for directions.'

156

A kangaroo enters a café and orders an iced tea.
The barman looks surprised, but serves him an iced tea.
'That's 25 dollars, please,' says the barman.
After a while, the barman says,
'You're the first kangaroo I've seen in my café!'
'No wonder,' says the kangaroo.
'If you charge 25 dollars for an iced tea!'

157

A camel asks his mother, 'Why do we have such flat feet?'
'So we don't fall over when we're walking through
the dusty sand in the desert, darling.'
'And why do we have such long eyelashes?'
'To keep the desert sand out of our eyes.'
'And why do we have such big humps?'
'The humps store reserves of food,
so that we don't get hungry in the desert.'
The young camel thinks for a while and says,
'Mummy, if that's all for the desert,
what are we doing here in the zoo?'

Emily goes to a hamburger restaurant with her father.
'Dad, I need to tell you something,' says Emily.
'Not while we're eating,' her father replies. 'It's bad manners.
Tell me in a moment when I've finished my hamburger.'
When he finishes his hamburger, he turns to Emily and asks,
'What did you want to tell me so urgently just now?'
'That there was a worm in your hamburger, Dad.'

159

'What job does your father do?' the teacher asks Amelia.
'He's a magician,' replies Amelia.
'How interesting! What is his favourite trick?' asks the teacher.
'Sawing people in half,' replies Amelia.
'And do you have any brothers or sisters?' asks the teacher.
'Yes,' says Amelia, 'a half-brother and three half-sisters!'

A woman goes to the doctor.
'Doctor, my husband thinks he's a refrigerator!'
'Oh, that's not too serious, madam,' says the doctor.
'Yes, it is,' she replies. 'He sleeps with his mouth open
and the light keeps me awake!'

**What did the big chimney say
to the small chimney?**

'You're too little to smoke!'

'Why haven't you eaten your egg?' asks Aunt Milly.
'I didn't like the taste,' says Sandra.
'When I was your age, I would have been
very happy with that egg!' Aunt Milly replies.
'Perfectly understandable,' says Sandra.
'At least it would have been fresh then!'

What is black and white and eats like a horse?

A zebra.

'Why is your dog looking at me like that while I'm eating?'
asks Benjamin.
'Because you're eating out of his bowl!'

**What happens when you throw
a black cat into the Red Sea?**

It gets wet.

Daniel takes his old, clapped out car to the garage.
'A mirror for my car, please,' he says to the mechanic.
'OK,' says the mechanic. 'That's a pretty good exchange!'

Three friends make a bet. They go to the top of a mountain and throw their watches off. The idea is to run to the bottom as fast as possible and get there before the watch hits the ground. The first friend runs down, but finds his watch in a thousand pieces.

The second friend throws his watch and chases down the mountain, but arrives at the bottom too late, to find his watch smashed to smithereens. The third friend throws his watch down, strolls leisurely to the bottom and drinks a can of lemonade when he gets there. Then he reaches into the air and catches his watch!

'However did you do that?' ask his friends in amazement.

'My watch is an hour behind!' he replies.

165

If a plane were to crash on the border between Switzerland and Italy, where would the survivors be buried?

Nowhere – you'd only bury the dead.

Giles comes home from school and his mother asks,
'How was your first day at school?'
'First day?' he replies. 'You mean I have to go back
again tomorrow?!'

What is worse than finding
a worm in your apple?

Finding half a worm in your apple.

Two men are having a drink in a pretty grotty bar.
The waiter asks, 'And what would you like to drink?'
'A cola, please,' says one man.
'For me too,' says the other,
'But could you put it in a clean glass, please?'
A little later the waiter returns with two glasses of cola.
'So, who ordered the clean glass?'

168

Mark asks Gavin, 'Does your dad always snore?'
'No,' replies Gavin. 'Only when he's asleep.'

How do you stop your dog from digging holes in your garden?

Take away his spade.

Bert is walking down the street with Derrick.
'Hey, look at that!' Bert shouts. 'A dead bird!'
'Where?' asks Derrick, looking up.

170

What do you call a penguin in the desert?

Lost!

171

Why are animals with 4 legs not good at dancing?

Because they have two left feet.

Parents are never happy: when you make noise, they tell you to be quiet and when you're quiet, they stick a thermometer in your mouth!

172

Two crows are sitting on a branch.
Suddenly a fighter jet flies over.
One crow says to the other: 'He's going fast!'
The other replies:
'Well, I'd like to see how you'd fly with your tail on fire!'

What car do small people drive?

A Mini Cooper!

Dave and Dylan come across a glass wall while out walking.
'May I stand on your shoulders?' asks Dave.
'Why?' asks Dylan.
'So I can see what's on the other side.'

Why do firemen wear red braces?

To keep their trousers up!

A kiwi and an egg are sitting in the doctor's waiting room.
The kiwi asks the egg: 'So, when is the plaster cast coming off?'

Lee is playing with his brother Nick in his room.
Nick wants to be the boss. 'Okay,' says Lee.
'You can be the boss if I can decide what we'll do!'

What washes up on very small beaches?

Microwaves.

Cowboy Bob buys a new horse. The horse seller tells him
that the horse can follow a few basic commands.
'Say "Trot" if you want him to trot, "My" if you want him
to sprint and "Whoa" if you want him to stop.'
The cowboy pays the man and rides off into the sunset on
his new acquisition. After a while, he decides to test the horse.
'My,' he says, and the horse immediately starts to sprint. Charging
at full speed, the cowboy looks ahead in horror as they approach
a vast gorge. 'WHOA!!!' he shouts, at the top of his lungs.
The horse stops within a metre of the edge of a deep drop.
'My, my, that was close,' sighs the cowboy and
the horse sprints straight into the ravine.

A clown visits a doctor. The doctor asks what's wrong,
to which the clown replies:
'Doctor, I've been feeling a little funny lately.'

What did the hedgehog
say to the cactus?

Are you my mother?

'Isn't it boring being married to an archaeologist?'
Jessie asks Paula.
'Not at all. The older I get, the more interesting he thinks I am!'

What is the difference between a flea and a dog?

A dog can have fleas, but a flea can't have dogs!

'Dad, there is a man at the door collecting
for the new swimming pool.'
'Give him a glass of water!'

Two fools want to make a fire. One fool says to the other:
'Are you sure that the matches work?'
The other replies: 'Yes, I've tried them all
to be sure they work!'

181

What did the skeleton say in the café?

'I'll have an orange juice and a mop please!'

What has no beginning, no end and nothing in the middle?

A doughnut!

182

What is the definition of an optimist?

Someone who buys hair growth lotion
from a bald hairdresser.

What goes up a drainpipe, down, but won't go down a drainpipe, up?

An umbrella.

'Would you like something to eat?' the stewardess asks a passenger. The man replies: 'Yes, please. What is there to choose from?' To which the stewardess replies: 'From yes or no.'

'You've made 20 mistakes in your assignment, Charlotte,
and the strange thing is that your neighbour has made exactly
the same ones! How do you explain that?' asks the teacher.
Charlotte thinks for a while and answers:
'I think it's because we have the same teacher!'

185

What happens if you leave
a diamond in water for too long?

It gets wet.

A hedgehog crosses a car park
and sees a car with a flat tyre.
'Finally,' he sighs, 'a hedgehog won.'

'Why do you keep talking to yourself?'
'Because then I know I'll get a sensible answer.'

Jeff walks up to his boss and says,
'Why do you want to fire me? I haven't done anything.'
'Exactly!' snorts his boss.

**What has an eye
but can't see?**

A needle!

188

Louise is playing a lullaby on the piano.
'Stop that right now,' complains her mother.
'You'll wake the baby!'

189

'What are you up to?' asks Mum.
'I'm writing a letter to Timmy,' replies Greg.
'Why are you writing so slowly?'
'Because Timmy can't read very fast.'

'Elise says to Marty, 'I wish I lived in the Middle Ages.'
Marty asks, 'Why's that?'
'So I wouldn't have to have so many history lessons.'

Two grains of sand are walking in the desert.
One says to the other:
'I think we're being followed.'

'Are you superstitious?'
'No.'
'Can you lend me 13 pounds then?'

What should you take
before each meal?

A chair!

~~~~~~~

A conductor is checking tickets on a train
that has been delayed for a long time.
'But sir,' says the conductor, 'that is a child's ticket.'
'Yes, you can imagine how long I've been waiting in this train!'
replies the man.

192

A boat is sailing down the street. A man passing on his bike says to the captain, 'Hey, you should sail on water, not on the street!'
But the captain ignores him and carries on sailing.
The cyclist meets a policeman further on. 'Excuse me officer, there's a man sailing down the street in a boat back there.'
The officer replies, 'Oh, I'll swim down there straightaway then!'

193

'Thomas, did you give the goldfish new water?'
'No, Mum, he hadn't finished yesterday's yet!'

Eli goes to school for the first day.
The teacher asks, 'Eli, do you know the alphabet?'
'Yes, miss!' Eli replies.
'Which letter comes after A?'
'All of them, miss!'

Why do giraffes have
long necks?

So they can't smell their feet.

Two flies come out of a cinema.
It's raining buckets and one flea says to the other flea:
'What shall we do? Shall we go by foot or by dog?'

'When we can see through something,
we say that it's transparent,' says the teacher.
'Can someone give me an example?'
Jacob answers, 'A keyhole, sir!'

196

Liam's mum places a bowl of soup on the table in front of him and says, 'I've just washed this tablecloth, so don't dirty it! Otherwise I'll deduct two pounds from your pocket money for every stain you make.' Then she goes back into the kitchen. When she returns, she sees Liam spreading soup over the tablecloth with his spoon. Furious, she shouts, 'Liam! What in heaven's name are you doing?' Liam says, 'Turning three stains into one.'

197

What did the 9 say to the 6?

'Have you fallen over?'

Why is a black chicken smarter than a white chicken?

Because a black chicken can lay white eggs,
but a white chicken can't lay black ones!

Why are bananas curved?

Because otherwise they wouldn't fit in your lunch box.

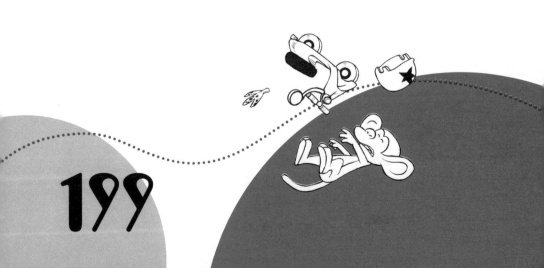

Why do chicks come out of eggs?

Because they're afraid of being cooked in them.

A father and son are walking along the coast.
The son says to his father, 'Look Dad, a boat.'
'That's not a boat,' his father replies. 'It's a hovercraft!'
'A hovercraft? How do you spell that?' asks the boy.
'Umm… sorry,' says his father, 'you were right, it's a boat!'

200

Caleb is in a drawing lesson.
The teacher asks him why he hasn't drawn anything yet.
Caleb replies, 'I have drawn something – a grazing cow.'
The teacher replies, 'But I don't see any grass!'
'The cow ate it,' replies Caleb.
'But I don't see a cow!' says the teacher, baffled.
Caleb replies, 'You don't really think the cow would stay there
if there's no more grass?'

Which animal can jump higher than a house?

All animals – houses can't jump!

Ella asks Norbit, 'Do you always pray before eating?'
'No,' replies Norbit, 'my mum's a great cook!'

202

Which tree doesn't have any leaves?

A family tree.

Anna returns home from the dentist.
'Does your tooth still hurt?' her dad asks her.
'I don't know,' replies Anna,
'the dentist kept it.'

Joshua walks into the kitchen.
'Mum, Mum, the ladder in the lounge has fallen over!'
Mum replies, 'Wait until Dad hears that!'
'He already knows,' says Joshua,
'he's hanging from the chandelier!'

205

'I haven't slept for days.'
'Why's that?'
'Because I always sleep in the nighttime!'

A snail spots a slug passing by:
'Wow! A convertible!'

'How did you manage to stop smoking?'
'I went to work in a fireworks factory.'

207

~~~~~

Charlie arrives late in class.
His teacher askes: 'Why are you late, Charlie?'
'I was dreaming about football!' replies Charlie.
Surprised by his answer, his teacher replies:
'That's no reason to be late, is it?'
To which Charlie replies:
'But miss, the game had overtime!'

What is a witch's favourite subject in school?

Spelling.

Two mosquitoes are on a bicycle ride.
One mosquito is wearing glasses.
'Why are you wearing glasses?'
asks the other mosquito.
'Because then at least I won't get
any insects in my eyes!'

209

An elephant stumbles into a pharmacy.
'Four metres of plasters, please.'
'Four metres?!'
'Yes, I walked through a porcelain cabinet.'

**What's the difference between
a cow and a centipede?**

996 legs.

'Do fish grow quickly, Mummy?'
'Ask your dad, love. He caught a carp
last week and every time he talks about it,
it gets 5 cm longer!'

Bart and Tom buy a bottle of lemonade.
'We can drink half each,' says Bart.
'Good idea,' replies Tom.
Bart brings the bottle up to his lips and guzzles
down every last drop.
'What are you doing?' asks Tom.
'My half was at the bottom,' replies Bart.

**What is white, light, square
and as big as a ping-pong ball?**

A ping-pong block.

Ryan and Max are playing dice.
When it's Max's turn,
he throws the dice against the ceiling.
'Why are you doing that?' asks Ryan.
'Because the person who throws
the highest is the winner, isn't he?'

213

A celebrity is someone who works hard
for years to become famous and,
when they finally get there,
wears dark glasses to avoid being recognised.

●●●●●●

What is small, yellow and square?

A small, yellow square.

A man is fishing.
After a while, a policeman approaches and says,
'Sir, you're not allowed to fish here!'
'Oh,' says the man, 'I'm not fishing.
I'm just teaching my worms to swim!'

215

'I've set a new record for the 100 metres!' shouts Jerry.
'Oh, what's the new record then?' asks his friend.
'102 metres!'

How do you stop an astronaut's baby from crying?

You rocket.

216

The teacher asks Leo:
'How many ribs does a human have?'
'I don't know,' replies Leo, 'I'm so ticklish
that I've never been able to count them!'

217

'Mum, what is a desert?' asks Carol.
'It's a bare expanse where nothing can grow,'
replies her mother.
'Oh, like Dad's head then?'

218

'Stop pulling silly faces at that bulldog, Henry!'
'He started it!'

219

'Why have you tied a knot in your hanky?'
'My mum did it, to remind me to post a letter.'
'So, have you posted it?'
'No, she forgot to give me the letter.'

220

Logan bets that he can eat 30 hotdogs.
However, he only manages 29.
'I wish I'd known,' he sighs.
'I'd have eaten the 30th first!'

221

Two cows are sitting in a bath.
One cow asks the other:
'Can you pass the soap?'
'Why?' asks the other cow.
'Because I'm covered in spots!'

222

**What's the best way to
make a bull sweat?**

Clothe him in a thick jumper.

223

Why do flamingoes always stand on one leg?

Because if they lifted the other, they'd fall over.

'Do you know how ostriches are born?'
'They come out of an egg.'
'And do you know how zebras are born?'
'Stripe by stripe.'

224

A rabbit is hopping happily past a petrol station.
He asks the petrol pump, 'Are you a robot?'
The petrol pump doesn't respond.
The rabbit asks again: 'Are you a robot or not?'
Irritated from receiving no response once again, he says,
'Hey, you! Take your fingers out of your ears!'

'What did you get for your birthday?'
'A trumpet – such a good investment.'
'Why's that?'
'Because I get a pound for every day
I leave it in the cupboard!'

Where will you find an ocean without water?

On a map.

226

Why did the chicken cross the road?

To get to the other side.

227

A man gets onto the bus
and asks the driver,
'Are you going to the zoo?'
'No,' says the bus driver,
'I have to work.'

'How's your new boss?'
'Terrible – you can't sleep at
your desk for a second!'
'Is that so strict?!'
'You don't understand;
she snores really loudly!'

'How old are you?'
'Six.'
'And what do you want to be when you're older?'
'Seven.'

230

Why did Mickey Mouse go into space?

Because he wanted to see Pluto.

231

'Evan, if you have seven apples in your left hand
and five in your right, what do you have?'
'Big hands, miss.'

What has 2 eyes and 100 teeth?

A crocodile.

What has 100 eyes and 2 teeth?

A bus full of old people.

A policeman patrolling the streets sees
a man thrashing around in a castle moat.
The man shouts, 'Help, help, officer, I can't swim!'
'Ah, that's OK then,' says the policeman,
'because you're not allowed to swim here!'

233

What kind of tree fits in your hand?

A palm tree.

What animal is always at a baseball game?

A bat.

234

**Why did the computer
have to go to the doctor?**

Because it had a virus.

235

♥

Little Bruno has been examined
with a stethoscope by the doctor.
When he arrives home, his father asks what the doctor did.
'Oh, it was fun, Daddy,' replies the boy.
'The doctor telephoned my tummy!'

〰〰〰

Two snails are sitting at the side of the road.
One snail says to the other, 'I'm going to cross over.'
'No, don't!' shouts the other.
'There's a bus coming in two hours!'

237

What is black and white and makes a lot of noise?

A zebra with a drum kit.

What is small, soft and slightly purple?

A koala holding its breath!

'Dad, where is Africa?'
asks Louise.
'Ask Mum,' replies Dad.
'She always knows where to find things.'

239

The teacher is marking homework.
'Stuart, you've got everything right.
Did you do this with your dad?'
'No miss, he did it on his own this time!'

Why did the astronauts go to a computer store?

To hang out at the spacebar.

240

A married couple goes on holiday,
only to find that all the hotels are full.
Finally they find a small hotel on the outskirts of the city.
'I have a vacant room for you,' says the manager,
'but the bed isn't made yet.'
'Oh, that's not a problem,' says the woman. 'I can do that myself.'
'OK,' replies the manager, surprised.
'Here is some wood and a hammer.'

What did the digital clock say to the grandfather clock?

'Look Grandpa, no hands!'

What kind of table
doesn't have any legs?

The times table.

'I've bought a present for Dad that he won't
be able to wear all at the same time,'
Richard tells his mum.
'That must be a huge present, love.
What is it?' she asks.
'Two ties!' Richard replies.

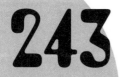

243

**When do you go through red
and stop at green?**

When you're eating a watermelon.

In a fish and chip shop.
'What would you like, sir?'
'Chips, please.'
'With pleasure, sir!'
'No, with tomato sauce!'

A rabbit goes to the bakery and asks,
'Do you have any carrot cake?'
To which the baker replies, 'No, I don't. Sorry.'
A day later the rabbit returns to the bakery and asks again:
'Do you have any carrot cake today?'
The baker replies: 'No, I don't have any carrot cake today.'
But the baker decides to make carrot cake especially
for the rabbit. The next day the rabbit returns and asks,
'Do you have any carrot cake?'
'Yes, I do,' says the baker proudly.
'Disgusting, isn't it?' says the rabbit.

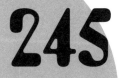

If you had four pounds in your pocket and you lost two, what would you have in your pocket?

A hole!

~~~~~~

What goes all round the world, but sticks in the corner?

A stamp.

246

'How long were you away on holiday for?'
'Ten minutes on my skis and three weeks in hospital.'

247

'Which animal excels at adapting?' asks the teacher.
Luke answers, 'Chickens, sir!'
'What makes you say that?' replies the teacher.
'Well, they lay eggs that fit into cups!'

248

Tyler and Andrew are at a red light.
Suddenly, Tyler says, 'It's green!'
to which Andrew replies, 'A frog?'

How do you talk to a giant?

By using big words.

'Mum, do you know why fish don't talk?' asks Johnny.
'No,' answers his mother. 'Because they're afraid they'll swallow
too much water when they open their mouths!'

250

Owen sees a car with two penguins on the back seat at
the traffic lights. 'Hey, sir, you need to take them to the zoo!'
'OK, will do!' says the man. A week later Owen sees the car
again, with the same two penguins on the back seat.
He walks to the car and says to the driver,
'I thought you were taking them to the zoo?'
'Yes, I did,' he replies.
'Today we're going to the amusement park!'

What's the difference between a swallow and a parrot?
A swallow needs to find his way on his own,
while a parrot can ask for directions.

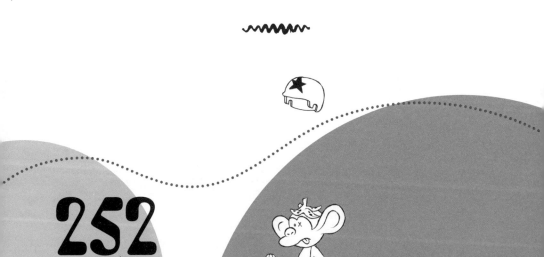

252

An explorer meets a medicine man in the jungle,
who is beating hard on a drum.
'What's wrong?' asks the explorer.
'We have no water,' replies the medicine man.
'Ah, so you're doing a rain dance?'
'No,' replies the medicine man.
'I'm trying to wake the plumber.'

What's the difference between a dentist and a teacher?

A dentist says, 'open your mouth,' and a teacher says, 'close your mouth!'

254

A man is walking through the mountains and suddenly
sees a lumberjack chopping down a beautiful, big tree.
'Why are you doing that?' asks the man.
'Because we're going to have a very hard winter,' he replies.
'How do you know that?'
'Do you see the old man at the top of that mountain?
We always get a hard winter when he stands there.'
'Then I'd like to speak to him,' says the man.
On reaching the mountain top, he asks the old man, 'Sir,
how do you know that we're going to have a very hard winter?'
'Do you see that lumberjack down there? Well, when he chops
down big trees, it means we're going to have a hard winter.'

255

What is red and goes up and down?

A tomato in a lift.

•••••••

What's blue and flies through the trees?

Tarzan in the winter.

A centipede arrives late for class.
'Why are you late?' asks the teacher.
'It's not my fault,' says the centipede.
'There's a sign outside saying "wipe your feet"!'

257

A mother gets into a lift with her children
in a department store. She presses the button
for the children's department and
one of her children says,
'No, Mum. Not another one.
There's already six of us.'

258

Jasper and Isabelle are driving to the beach.
Jasper keeps driving through red traffic lights.
'What are you doing?' asks Isabelle.
'My brother always does the same,' replies Jasper.
Suddenly he stops at a green light.
'But what are you doing now?' asks Isabelle, panicking.
'Well, imagine what would happen if my brother
were to come from the other direction!'

259

**What happened to the monster
who took the 5 o'clock train?**

He had to give it back.

Charlie and Peter are waiting
on opposite sides of the street.
Charlie calls to Peter, 'I need to cross
over to the other side!'
'Why?' says Peter, 'you're already there!'

Anthony is stopped by the police on the motorway.
'Sir,' says the officer, 'do you realise that you were
driving at 140 miles an hour?'
'That's not possible,' replies Anthony.
'I've only had my car for half an hour!'

261

A man on death row is asked
if he has one last wish.
'Yes,' is his reply.
'I'd like to learn to play the piano.'

~~~~~~

**Which side of a chicken
has the most feathers?**

The outside.

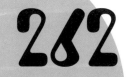

262

Derrick and Fred are driving their lorry
under a bridge when the top of the lorry catches
the underside of the bridge and they get stuck.
Two policemen stop next to the lorry and tell them
to let their tyres down to create ten centimetres.
'That won't help,' says Derrick.
'The lorry is stuck at the top!'

What do you need to know
to become a lion tamer?

More than the lion.

When you know what I am,
I won't exist anymore. What am I?

A riddle.

264

Natalie goes for her first day in Year 3 at primary school,
where she is told she will learn to read and write.
In the evening her dad comes home from work
and asks what she has learnt.
'Well,' says Natalie, 'I learnt to write.'
'And what did you write?' asks Dad.
'I don't know yet. The reading lesson is tomorrow.'

265

Why did the elephant paint his toenails?

So that he could play hide-and-seek with the strawberries.

'This steak is old and tough, waiter!'
'Indeed, sir, which proves beyond a doubt that
we only serve meat from animals that
were so healthy they reached a ripe old age!'

Casper says to his father,
'Dad, there's a salesman with a moustache at the door.'
His dad replies, 'Tell him I already have one.'

267

A boy sees a bee for the first time
in his life and shouts,
'Look, Mummy, that fly has put on
a striped sweater!'

**What did the 0
say to the 8?**

Nice belt!

'I always take my ruler with me to bed at night.'
'Whatever for?'
'To measure how long I sleep for, of course.'

269

What goes up
and never comes down?

Your age.

Name two animals that
live in the North Pole.

A polar bear and his wife.

270

'Waiter, I ordered my steak three times
but I still haven't received anything!'
The waiter turns to the kitchen and shouts,
'Where are sir's three steaks?'

271

'Granddad, may I have a sip of your beer?' asks Shaun.
'Wait until you're older!' replies Granddad.
'But it'll be long gone by then!' says Shaun.

Two fish are swimming in a fish bowl.
One says to the other:
'May I swim by the window for a change?'

A mother walks through the zoo with her daughter.
They arrive at the monkey enclosure and the little girl says,
'Hey, that monkey looks just like Uncle Gerry.'
Her mother replies, 'You can't say that!'
To which her daughter replies, 'Why?
The monkey can't hear me!'

273

'I will ask you two questions,' said the teacher.
'If you can guess the answer to the first question,
you don't have to answer the second.'
'How many hairs does a cow have?'
The class is silent. After a lot of thought, a boy raises his hand.
'33,967,234, sir!' he says.
'How did you arrive at that number?' asks the teacher, surprised.
'That's the second question, sir, so I don't need to answer it!'

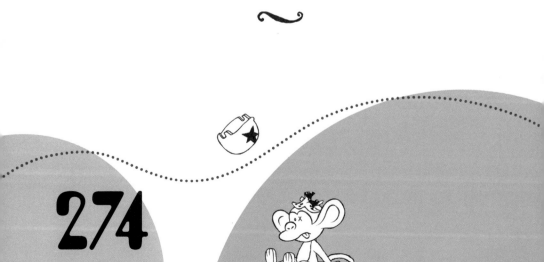

274

A couple is having dinner at a fish restaurant.
'What a shame we didn't discover this restaurant
a week ago,' says the man.
'Why, dear?' asks the woman.
'Would the food have tasted the same then, do you think?'
'No, but the fish would have been fresh!'

275

Robert is overweight. He goes to the doctor.
The doctor tells him, 'You need to lose a few pounds.
Try eating dry bread for a week'.
'Before or after the meal?' asks Robert.

Why do fish swim in salt water?

Because pepper makes them sneeze.

The teacher says to Jordan,
'You have to wash your face better;
I can see what you had for breakfast this morning!'
Jordan: 'What was it then?'
Teacher: 'Scrambled eggs.'
Jordan: 'Wrong, sir, that was yesterday.'

'I'm so clever,' says a girl to the shop assistant.
'I'm only six and I can write my name
front to back and back to front!'
'That's impressive!' replies the lady. 'What's your name then?'
'Anna!'

278

Caroline is eating a big blob of jam,
which she scooped out of the jar with her fingers.
Her mother catches her and says, angrily,
'I don't like that, young lady!'
'That's odd, Mummy, because I love it!'

279

Jake asks his mum to put a spoonful
of sugar in his hot milk.
'But Jake, you've already had four spoonfuls!'
'Yes, Mum, but they've melted!'

**When can you get an elephant, a rhinoceros
and a giraffe under the same umbrella
without them getting wet?**

When it's not raining!

281

♥

Why do dentists only ask whether it hurts
when you can't answer?

Rick finds a 5 pound note on the floor.
'What are you going to do with the money?' asks his friend.
'Buy a wallet to put the note in,' answers Rick.

282

Conner asks the teacher,
'Sir, can I be punished for something I haven't done?'
to which the teacher replies, 'Of course not.'
'Thank goodness,' says Conner.
'Because I haven't done my homework!'

283

'I can't sleep when I drink coffee!' says Harry to his friend Mike.
'It's the other way round for me,' says Mike.
'I can't drink coffee when I sleep!'

284

A man is having his beard trimmed at the barber's.
But the barber is working so slowly that the man is starting
to get agitated. 'Could you trim it a little faster, perhaps?'
he grumbles. 'I can feel the right side of my beard starting
to grow again while you're trimming the left!'

285

A man eating in a restaurant in the mountains
summons the waiter: 'Dear man,
I ordered a steak and you've brought me three?'
'My apologies, sir,' replies the waiter,
'It's that blooming echo here!'

286

Two cows are standing in a meadow.
Suddenly one starts to shake violently.
'What on Earth are you doing?' asks the other.
'It's my birthday tomorrow,' replies the shaking cow.
'So I thought I'd make some whipped cream for the cake.'

Leo tells his girlfriend,
'I can't eat in the morning because I'm thinking of you.
I can't eat in the afternoon because I'm thinking of you.
I can't eat in the evening because I'm thinking of you.'
'And at night?'
'I can't sleep because I'm hungry!'

A man arrives at a party and asks the hostess
if he can come in. 'Of course,' says the woman.
'But I have dirty feet,' says the man.
'That's alright,' replies the woman.
'You're wearing shoes, aren't you?'

289

Aria says to Bert, 'My dream is to earn
a million pounds a month, just like Daddy!'
'Does your dad earn a million pounds a month?'
asks Bert, impressed.
'No,' says Aria, 'but he dreams of it too!'

A man and a woman are walking through a museum.
'What an ugly work of art,' says the woman.
'Put your glasses on, love,' says the man,
'you're looking at a mirror!'

291

Riley calls the plumber.
'Is your house really damp then?'
'Yes, it's terrible! There were fish
caught in the mouse trap this morning!'

♥

A policeman is walking down a street and sees
a small girl trying unsuccessfully to reach a doorbell.
Wanting to assist, he helps by pressing the bell.
The girl looks up and says,
'Thanks! Now we have to run away really fast!'

293

John is walking his rabbit down the street.
His highly bemused neighbour asks him where
the rabbit sleeps. 'In my bedroom!' answers John.
'Really?' asks the neighbour, 'doesn't it smell awful?'
'Yes, but he'll get used to that!'

What did the slug sitting
on the tortoise's back say?

'Not so fast!'

Two ships have collided and the captains
are arguing about whose fault it was.
'The mist was so thick that I could hardly
tie my shoelaces!' says one.
'There you have it!' says the other.
'If you hadn't been tying your shoelaces,
you wouldn't have sailed into me!'

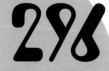

Both of Cedric's ears are burning.
His friend asks, 'How come your ears are burning?'
'Well, I was ironing my clothes and
the telephone rang!' says Cedric.
'But why are both your ears burning then?' asks his friend.
'Because I had to call the doctor, too.'

Jaden goes to the zoo with his dad.
When they arrive at the lions' den, Jaden asks,
'Why do lions have such big heads, Dad?'
'Think about it carefully, boy,' replies his father.
'Ah, I know!' says Jaden, 'To prevent them from
getting through the bars on the fence!'

How do you keep an idiot occupied all day?

By writing 'please turn over' on both sides of a piece of paper before giving it to him.

'How much is that pan?' asks Ted.
'Thirty pounds, sir,' replies the shop assistant.
'Wow, that much… Could you take something off, perhaps?'
'Yes, the lid!'

Mother: 'Jackson, could you nip out and do the shopping
with your sister? Here is the shopping list – and stick to it!'
Jackson does the shopping but leaves his sister alone in the shop.
When Jackson arrives home a little later,
his mother asks, 'Where is your sister?'
'At the shop,' Jackson replies.
'Well, why didn't you bring her home?!'
'Because she wasn't on the list, Mum.'

Two flies are sitting on a cowpat.
One says to the other: 'I know a good joke.'
The other replies: 'As long as it's not dirty;
I'm having my dinner.'

301

What gets wetter the more it dries?

A towel.

How do hedgehogs play leapfrog?

Very carefully!

'Nellie, what on Earth are you doing?
You're sitting in front of the mirror with your eyes closed...?'
'Yes, Mum, I want to see what my face looks like
when I'm sleeping!'

'Why are you whining so much?'
the dentist asks his patient,
'I haven't started drilling yet!'
'No, but you're standing on my toes!'

'Look, Granddad, I've made a castle
from bricks,' says Noah.
'But Noah, the bricks are just scattered on the floor.'
'That's right,' beams Noah, 'it's a ruin!'

'Flynn, can you open the door when the headmaster arrives?'
'Who is the headmaster?' asks Flynn.
'That's the man who can do anything,' replies the teacher.
'Why can't he open the door himself then?'

306

'How did you get that bump
on your forehead, Ella?' asks her mother.
'The boy next door threw water at me!' Ella replies.
'But that wouldn't give you a bump,' Mum objects.
'Yes, it would. The water was still in a bottle!'

Why are goldfish orange?

Because the water makes them rust!

'I know someone who hasn't had
their hair cut in 15 years!' says Gerald.
'Wow, I bet that's quite a sight!' says Benny.
'It's OK, actually,' replies Gerald,
'he's been bald for the past 15 years!'

Grandma has had her hair cut very short.
When her grandson sees her, he says,
'Grandma, you don't look like an old woman anymore.'
Grandma beams and replies,
'Thank you, love. How do I look then?'
'Like an old man!' says the boy.

'You can swim very well!'
said Billy to a small, 6-year-old boy in the swimming pool.
'Yes, I've been swimming since I was 3!' said the boy.
'Wow, you must be tired then!'

311

'Mum, do all fairy tales start with "once upon a time"?'
'Yes,' Mum replies, 'Except yours, of course;
yours start with "Honestly, Mum, I didn't do anything!"'

312

Two fortune tellers meet at the market.
One says to the other: 'You look better than tomorrow!'

313

What is full of holes but can still hold water?

A sponge.

What is a tornado's favourite game to play?

Twister.

314

A puppy asks his father,
'Daddy, what is my name exactly,
"Sit" or "Lie"?'

315

'Dear Lord,' prays Walter before going to bed,
'please make Rome the capital of Germany.'
'Walter, dear,' interrupts his mother,
'why are you asking the Lord to do something like that?!'
'Because that's the answer I gave in my geography test today!'

316

The mother of a young mosquito asks her son,
'So, how was your first flight?'
'It was fantastic and the people were really nice –
every time I flew past, they clapped their hands!'

Will asks a hunter, 'Why do you close one eye
when aiming your gun?'
The hunter replies, 'Because if I closed both,
I wouldn't be able to see anything!'

What is the same size as a giraffe, but weighs nothing?

Its shadow!

319

An old woman gets onto a bus and gives the bus driver a bag of peanuts. The driver thanks the woman and gobbles them up.
'Thanks, but why did you give me the peanuts?' he asks.
'Because I don't like them,' replies the woman.
'Why did you buy them then?' asks the driver.
'Because I do like the chocolate around them!'

320

Daisy goes to buy pizza. The cook asks her,
'Would you like me to slice the pizza into four for you? Or eight?'
'Four please,' replies Daisy, 'I'll never manage to eat eight!'

321

A woman goes to the doctor. 'What can I do for you?' he asks.
'Nothing for me, Doctor. I've come about my husband.'
'What is wrong with your husband?' asks the doctor.
'He thinks he's invisible.'
'Ask him to come and see me, madam,' instructs the doctor.
'But he's standing right next to you!'

**When you lie they stand up and
when you stand they lie flat on the ground.
What are they?**

Your toes.

323

'Why are you wearing glasses?' Victor says,
'you're better looking when you're not wearing them!'
Marni replies, 'That's odd, you're better looking
when I'm not wearing them as well!'

'John, why do you give your chickens
boiling water?' asks George.
'I want to see whether they can lay boiled eggs!'

Timothy asks Ronald,
'Did you hear about the fool
that keeps going around saying "no"?'
'No,' answers Ronald.
'Oh, so it's you!'

Michelle is knitting a jumper for her sister's birthday.
'Why are you knitting so fast?' asks her father.
'I want to finish the jumper before the wool runs out,'
replies Michelle.

'Nadia, have you seen your brother?'
'Yes, I put him in the fridge.'
'Have you lost your mind?! He'll catch a chill!'
'Don't worry, Mum, I closed the door!'

One girl asks another: 'Are you still
in love with that parachutist?'
'No, I dropped him!'

329

What is a volcano?

A big mountain with hiccups!

Why do divers fall backwards into the water?

Because if they fell forwards
they'd end up face down in the boat!

331

A dog and a giraffe go for a swim.
'Come into the water!' shouts the giraffe.
'It's not too deep; I can stand here
and the water only barely reaches my chin!'

332

What mustn't you forget to do before blowing out a candle?

Light it!

How do you cut a wave in half?

Using a sea-saw.

Two police officers are standing at a corner.
One officer asks the other:
'Can you check if the flashing light is still on?'
The other replies:
'Yes! No! Yes! No! Yes!'

334

Andy's dad tells him, 'You have to eat all your spinach
if you want to be as strong as Dad!'
'I don't want to be as strong as you,' says Andy,
'I want to be the boss, like Mum!'

335

'I'm never going into that shop again!' Will says to his friend.
'Last week the power went off in there and
we got stuck on the escalator for three hours!'

How do you write blue
with a black pen?

By beginning with 'b'.

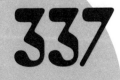

337

Why are rabbits in bed so early?

They only have two teeth to brush!

338

What is a skeleton in a cupboard?

A person who won a game of hide-and-seek 100 years ago.

Who prefers giving to receiving?

Boxers!

339

Evaline: 'I don't want to eat lettuce!'
Mum: 'But it's full of vitamins,
which will give your cheeks a lovely colour!'
Evaline: 'But I don't want green cheeks!'

340

'What is 6 minus 2?' asks the teacher.
'I don't know,' replies Tony.
'What do you get if there are six biscuits
in the bowl and you take two away?'
'A clip 'round the ear, miss!'

341

~mmmm~

What has 4 legs but can't walk?

A chair.

**Where does Superman do
his grocery shopping?**

In the supermarket!

What did one wall say to the other wall?

'Go stand in the corner.'

343

Teacher: 'What is the furthest:
America or the Moon?'
Jack: 'America, sir.'
Teacher: 'Why do you say that?'
Jack: 'Because at night I can see the Moon,
but not America.'

Who walked into a bear's den and walked out again alive?

The bear.

345

Mr Dickens arrives at a hotel and asks for a room.
'I'm sorry, sir,' the hotel manager says,
'but we are fully booked; there are no free rooms.'
'And what if the Queen needed a room?' Mr Dickens replies.
'For the Queen we would always find a room,'
says the hotel manager.
'Well, luckily for me the Queen isn't coming,' Mr Dickens says,
'so you can give me the room you kept available for her.'

346

**What would you do if you were standing
eye-to-eye with a lion and a jaguar?**

Jump into the Jaguar and drive away!

347

'I don't need a clock to know what time it is at night,'
Steve proudly says in class.
'How do you do that?' the teacher asks.
'I just take my trumpet outside and play a tune,'
Steve replies, 'Within two minutes my dad yells,
"Get back to bed, it's 3 a.m.!"'

348

'Dear, why did you get out of bed so early this morning?'
Gwen asks her husband.
'You know the rooster died yesterday,' her husband replies,
'well, someone had to wake the chicken.'

349

'Philip, can you name me three animals
that live in Africa?' the teacher asks.
'That's easy, sir,' Philip replies,
'a lion and her two cubs.'

Mason goes to the doctor and says,
'Doctor, I think I need glasses.'
'I think you're probably right,' replies Nick.
'You're at a shoe shop!'

351

Belle comes home early from her first day at cookery school
and says, 'I got kicked out of school.'
'Whatever for?' her sister asks, surprised.
'I burnt something in class.'
'Everyone burns something every now and then
when they're learning to cook,' her sister replies.
'I know,' Belle says, 'but apparently not everyone
burns down the entire classroom.'

352

'Did you know that you need three sheep
to make one woolly sweater?' Jacky asks Madge.
Madge replies: 'Wow, I didn't even know sheep could knit!'

353

At the breakfast table Benjamin asks,
'Mummy, what did I do in my dream last night?'
'I don't know, dear,' Mummy replies.
'Daddy, can you tell me what I did?'
'How would I know, son?' Daddy asks.
'I don't understand,' the little boy says, confused,
'I'm sure you both were there.'

'Uncle Frank, how fast does the Earth spin?'
Elijah asks.
'That depends on how much beer I had to drink.'

A tourist wants to take a dip in the river.
He asks his guide, 'Are there any sharks in this river?'
'No, sir.'
'And any crocodiles?'
'No, definitely not.'
Feeling assured, the tourist jumps into the river,
to which the guide replies, 'but I would watch out
for piranhas and sea snakes.'

356

One day Simon comes up to his dad and says:
'Dad, I'm getting married!'
Dad: 'To who?'
Simon: 'To Granny.'
Dad: 'That's not possible, son. Granny is my mother.'
Simon: 'So? You married my mother, didn't you?'

'Yes, I'm going to be rich!' Mikey tells his mum,
holding out the baby tooth he just lost.
'Why dear,' his mother replies, 'I don't think the tooth fairy will
give you that much for your baby tooth that you'll be rich.'
'No,' Mikey replies, 'but I'm talking about my golden tooth.'
'Which golden tooth?' his mother asks, confused.
'When Grandpa lost his tooth, he got a golden tooth, didn't he!'
Mikey says, confidently.

Suzy: 'Hey little brother! The chocolate smudges
on your face give away that you've already eaten from
the pudding! I'm telling Mum, and you won't get any dessert!'
Suzy's little brother: 'Go ahead,
you won't get any dessert either: I ate it all!'

Logan arrives at school an hour late.
'Why are you so late?' the headteacher demands.
'I fell from the stairs, sir,' Logan replies.
'For an entire hour?' the headteacher continues,
'that must have been one tall staircase!'

●●●●●●●

It's a sunny day and two angels
are making casual conversation.
'Do you know what weather it will be tomorrow?'
'Cloudy.'
'Great, we'll have a place to sit.'

361

Why are ghosts bad liars?

Because you can see right through them!

What do you call an alligator wearing a vest?

An investigator.

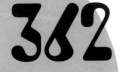

362

The teacher asks in class.
'What can you tell me about the Dead Sea, Ava?'
'Not much, miss,' Ava replies,
'I didn't even know it was sick.'

What has five fingers, but no hand?

A glove.

How do oceans say hello to each other?

They wave.

364

Olivia's mum is pregnant. She asks her daughter,
'Sweetheart, what would you prefer –
a little brother, or a little sister?'
'If it is all the same by you,' Olivia replies, 'I'd prefer a dog.'

365